TOP 10

POISONOUS ANIMALS

Children's Press®
An imprint of Scholastic Inc.

BY BRENNA MALONEY

A special thank-you to the Cincinnati Zoo & Botanical Garden for their expert consultation.

Library of Congress Cataloging-in-Publication Data available

ISBN 978-1-5461-7745-6 (library binding)
ISBN 978-1-5461-7746-3 (paperback)

10 9 8 7 6 5 4 3 2 1 26 27 28 29 30

Printed in China 62
First edition, 2026

Book design by Kay Petronio

Photos ©: back cover left, 2 left: sserg_dibrova/Getty Images; back cover right, 2 right: kikkerdirk/Getty Images; 4 top: Kim, Hyun-tae/iNaturalist; 4 center: TeleMakro Fotografie (Ina Hensel)/Getty Images; 4 bottom left: RainervonBrandis/Getty Images; 4 bottom right: Click48/Getty Images; 5 top left: Regent Vale/iNaturalist; 5 top right: Norbert Probst/imageBROKER.com/Alamy Images; 5 bottom left: Sara B. Weinstein; 5 bottom right: Gary Bell/Blue Planet Archive; 6 main: RainervonBrandis/Getty Images; 7: Georgette Douwma/Getty Images; 8–9: Trey Thomas/Getty Images; 10 inset: shutswis/Getty Images; 10–11: Kim, Hyun-tae/iNaturalist; 11 right: taek-guen-im/iNaturalist; 12–13: TeleMakro Fotografie (Ina Hensel)/Getty Images; 13 right: alan64/Getty Images; 14 inset: EHStock/Getty Images; 14–15: Click48/Getty Images; 15 right: Auscape/UIG/Shutterstock; 16 inset: skegbydave/Getty Images; 16–17: bnchapple/iNaturalist; 17 right: Sara B. Weinstein; 18–19: Regent Vale/iNaturalist; 19 right: Daniel Heuclin/Science Source; 20–21: Norbert Probst/imageBROKER.com/Alamy Images; 21 right: David Fleetham/Alamy Images; 23 right: Gary Nafis; 24–25: Gary Bell/Blue Planet Archive; 25 right: Gary Bell/Oceanwide/Minden Pictures; 26: Thomas Marent/Minden Pictures; 28–29: Thorsten Spoerlein/Getty Images; 29 inset: Patrick_Gijsbers/Getty Images; 30 top left: U.S. Fish & Wildlife Service; 30 bottom left: Vladimir Manaev/Dreamstime.com; 30 bottom center: David Fleetham/Alamy Images; 30 bottom right: Gary Bell/Blue Planet Archive. All other photos © Shutterstock.

CONTENTS

THE POWER OF POISON

ASIAN TIGER SNAKE

SPANISH FLY

HAWKSBILL TURTLE

CANE TOAD

Poison is something that can harm plants, animals, and humans. It can make them sick or even cause death! But did you know some animals use poison to survive? Poison can help animals catch **prey**.

It can also protect them from being eaten. Are you ready to learn which animal is the most poisonous? Read on and count down from ten to one. Let's learn which animal takes the top spot!

HOODED PITOHUI

ROUGH-SKINNED NEWT

PUFFERFISH

AFRICAN CRESTED RAT

GOLDEN POISON FROG

BLUE-RINGED OCTOPUS

#10 HAWKSBILL TURTLE

It might surprise you to see a turtle in this book. But the hawksbill sea turtle is poisonous! Hawksbills have sharp beaks. Their beaks chip away at coral reefs to eat. Sea sponges grow on coral reefs.

This turtle's favorite food is sea sponges. These sponges are poisonous. Eating them doesn't harm the turtles. But the poison stays in their bodies. A **predator** that eats a hawksbill can become very sick.

FACT
The hawksbill turtle has a pair of claws on each flipper.

HAWKSBILL TURTLE CLOSE-UP

SHELL

An oval shell has saw-like edges. It grows bigger as the turtle gets older.

SKIN

Golden-brown skin has streaks of orange, red, and black.

One hawksbill can eat more than 1,000 pounds (454 kg) of sea sponges per year. That is about the same weight as a rhinoceros!

BEAK
Its pointed beak can find food in small spaces.
EYES
Oval-shaped eyes see well underwater.
FLIPPERS
Flippers help it swim in the open ocean.

#9 ASIAN TIGER SNAKE

FACT FILE

ANIMAL GROUP: Reptile

HABITATS: Forests, ponds, small bodies of water

AVERAGE SIZE: A baseball bat

DIET: Carnivore

The Asian tiger snake is a master at self-defense. It eats poisonous frogs. Then it stores this poison in its body. The poison does not harm the snake.

When it's threatened, the poison comes out of its skin. But that's not all. This snake can also deliver **venom** through its bite! Venom is a type of poison injected into a wound.

FACT

Snakes can be born with poison in their bodies. The poison comes from their mothers.

#8 SPANISH FLY

FACT FILE

ANIMAL GROUP: Invertebrate

HABITATS: Fields, gardens, meadows

AVERAGE SIZE: A paper clip

DIET: Herbivore

The Spanish fly is not a fly. It's a beetle. And it is *very* poisonous. These beetles drip poison from their mouth and legs. Do not touch this beetle!

Your skin will get painful yellow blisters. The Spanish fly's poison can kill any animal that tries to eat it. Animals such as birds and **mammals** might eat this beetle by mistake.

FACT

The Spanish fly is a bright, shiny green color. This is a warning to stay away!

#7 CANE TOAD

FACT FILE

ANIMAL GROUP: **Amphibian**

HABITATS: Coastal grasslands, sand dunes

AVERAGE SIZE: Bigger than a baseball

DIET: Omnivore

Licking, biting, or eating a cane toad is a bad idea. These toads make a milky poison that covers their skin. This poison is thick and sticky.

The poison mainly comes from lumps on the toad's shoulders. They look like shoulder pads. A small amount of poison can sicken a wild animal, pet, or person.

FACT

Cane toad eggs and tadpoles are poisonous, too. Even *dead* cane toads are poisonous!

Cane toad eggs

Would a *rat* be on your list of poisonous animals? The African crested rat should be. These rats chew on the bark of poison arrow trees.

They mix the poison from that plant with their spit. Then they lick the striped hairs on their sides. If a predator tries to eat this rat, it will be poisoned!

FACT Hyenas and wild dogs are predators of the African crested rat.

#5 HOODED PITOHUI

(pee-toh-HOO-ee)

FACT FILE

ANIMAL GROUP: Bird

HABITAT: Rainforests

AVERAGE SIZE: An action figure

DIET: Omnivore

Pay attention to this bird's bright colors. Its skin and feathers are poisonous. Pitohuis become poisonous from the beetles they eat. The beetles' poison doesn't harm the birds. But it stays in their bodies.

Do not touch this bird! Its feathers carry the beetles' poison now. Your hand might tingle or feel numb. Your skin might burn. You might even start sneezing!

FACT The hooded pitohui is one of the few known poisonous birds.

#4 PUFFERFISH

FACT FILE

ANIMAL GROUP: Fish

HABITATS: Coasts, deep ocean, open waters, reefs

AVERAGE SIZE: Ranges from a screw to a golf club

DIET: Omnivore

Warning! Do NOT eat pufferfish. Their poison can be deadly! When threatened, these small fish try to make themselves look bigger. How? They quickly gulp water.

The water gets pumped into their stomachs. As their skin stretches, they also release a poison. It comes out through their skin. The poison can kill predators such as sharks.

FACT

Some types of pufferfish are even deadly to touch!

#3 ROUGH-SKINNED NEWT

FACT FILE

ANIMAL GROUP: Reptile

HABITATS: Lakes, ponds, slow-moving creeks, wetlands

AVERAGE SIZE: A butter knife

DIET: Carnivore

You might smell a rough-skinned newt before you see one. And that's a good thing. These newts give off a bad smell as a warning. It lets other animals know that they are poisonous.

That's not the only warning they give. When threatened, they rear their head and curl up their tail. They display their bright orange skin. This is a good time to run away!

FACT

Bacteria living on its skin make this newt poisonous.

#2 BLUE-RINGED OCTOPUS

FACT FILE

ANIMAL GROUP: Invertebrate

HABITATS: Coral reefs, tide pools

AVERAGE SIZE: A golf ball

DIET: Carnivore

The blue-ringed octopus is a dangerous ocean animal. It is both venomous and poisonous. It bites prey with its horny beak to inject venom.

The venom is made by bacteria in the octopus's mouth. The octopus's body is also poisonous. Touching this octopus can be deadly!

FACT

This octopus's blue rings will glow to warn predators.

The golden poison frog is the most poisonous animal on Earth! It eats poisonous insects.

The poison seeps through its skin. Touching a single frog can be deadly. One frog is poisonous enough to kill more than 20,000 mice. There is no cure for its poison.

FACT The golden poison frog is **endangered**.

EYES

Large, dark eyes help it to see in low light.

MOUTH

Bony, teeth-like plates in the upper jaw help grind its food.

FACT

This frog's poison has been used for hunting. It coats the tips of blow darts.

THROAT

Its throat swells when calling to other frogs.

TOES

Each foot has four toes for gripping.

GOLDEN POISON FROG CLOSE-UP

SKIN

This frog's most common skin color is deep yellow.

TONGUE

A long, sticky tongue captures prey.

LEGS

Slender legs are used for hopping on land.

SIZING THEM UP

There are many poisonous animals on Earth! Some make their own poisons. Others become poisonous from the plants or animals they eat. Poisons can be mild. They can also be deadly. Can you think of other poisonous animals? Create your own list!

GLOSSARY

amphibian (am-FIB-ee-uhn) a cold-blooded animal with a backbone that lives in water and breathes with gills when young

bacteria (bak-TEER-ee-uh) microscopic, single-celled living things that are everywhere and can either be useful or harmful

carnivore (KAHR-nuh-vor) an animal that eats meat

coral reef (KOR-uhl reef) a reef made of coral and other materials that have solidified into rock

endangered (en-DAYN-jurd) a plant or animal that is in danger of becoming extinct, usually because of human activity

herbivore (HUR-buh-vor) an animal that only eats plants

invertebrate (in-VUR-tuh-brit) an animal without a backbone

mammal (MAM-uhl) a warm-blooded animal that has fur and usually gives birth to live babies

omnivore (AHM-nuh-vor) an animal that eats both plants and meat

poison (POI-zuhn) a substance that can kill or harm a person, animal, or plant if it is swallowed, inhaled, absorbed, or touched

predator (PRED-uh-tur) an animal that lives by hunting other animals for food

prey (pray) an animal that is hunted by another animal for food

reptile (REP-tile) a cold-blooded animal that crawls across the ground or creeps on short legs; most have backbones and reproduce by laying eggs

venom (VEN-uhm) a poison that is injected through biting, clawing, or stinging

INDEX

Page numbers in **bold** indicate images.

ABOUT THE AUTHOR

Brenna Maloney is the author of many books. She lives in Washington, DC, with her husband and two sons. She was surprised to learn that birds and rats could be poisonous!